W9-AMN-018

Seals and Sea Lions

Debbie Gallagher

Marshall Cavendish
Benchmark
New York

This edition first published in 2010 in the United States of America by Marshall Cavendish Benchmark
An imprint of Marshall Cavendish Corporation

Website: www.marshallcavendish.us

This publication represents the opinions and views of the author based on Debbie Gallagher's personal experience, knowledge, and research. The information in this book serves as a general guide only. The author and publisher have used their best efforts in preparing this book and disclaim liability rising directly and indirectly from the use and application of this book.

Other Marshall Cavendish Offices:
Marshall Cavendish Ltd. 5th Floor, 32-38 Saffron Hill, London EC1N 8 FH, UK • Marshall Cavendish International (Asia) Private Limited, 1 New Industrial Road, Singapore 536196 • Marshall Cavendish International (Thailand) Co Ltd. 253 Asoke, 12th Flr, Sukhumvit 21 Road, Klongtoey Nua, Wattana, Bangkok 10110, Thailand • Marshall Cavendish (Malaysia) Sdn Bhd, Times Subang, Lot 46, Subang Hi-Tech Industrial Park, Batu Tiga, 40000 Shah Alam, Selangor Darul Ehsan, Malaysia

Marshall Cavendish is a trademark of Times Publishing Limited

All websites were available and accurate when this book was sent to press.

Library of Congress Cataloging-in-Publication Data

Gallagher, Debbie, 1969-
 Seals and sea lions / Debbie Gallagher.
  p. cm. — (Zoo animals)
 Includes index.
 Summary: "Discusses seals and sea lions, their natural habitat, behavior, characteristics, and zoo life"—Provided by publisher.
 ISBN 978-0-7614-4748-1
 1. Captive seals—Juvenile literature. 2. Seals (Animals)--Juvenile literature. 3. Sea lions—Juvenile literature. 4. Zoo animals—Juvenile literature. I. Title.
 SF408.6.S35G35 2010
 636.979—dc22

                              2009040078   1 3 5 6 4 2

First published in 2010 by
MACMILLAN EDUCATION AUSTRALIA PTY LTD
15–19 Claremont Street, South Yarra 3141

Visit our website at www.macmillan.com.au or go directly to www.macmillanlibrary.com.au

Associated companies and representatives throughout the world.

Copyright © Debbie Gallagher 2010

Edited by Georgina Garner
Text and cover design by Kerri Wilson
Page layout by Raul Diche
Photo research by Legend Images
Base maps by Gaston Vanzet, modified by Kerri Wilson

Printed in the United States

Acknowledgments
The author and the publisher are grateful to the following for permission to reproduce copyright material:

Front cover photo of California Sea Lions courtesy Photolibrary/ Egon Bömsch

Photographs courtesy of: AAP Image/Laura Friezer, **26** (right); Borås Djurpark Zoo, **12**, **22**, **23**; James Marshall/Corbis, **30**; © **Gnotzen**/Dreamstime.com, **26** (left); Cameron Spencer/ Getty Images, **27** (left); © Morten Elm/iStockphoto, **18**; © 2008 Jupiterimages Corporation, **4**; Legendimages, **24**, **25**, **27** (right); © **Masterfile**, **5**; © Newspix/News Ltd/David Caird, **21**; Photolibrary © FLPA/Alamy, **7**; Photolibrary/Egon Bömsch, **1**; Photolibrary/David B Fleetham, **10**; © Andrew Chin/Shutterstock, **8** (sea lion silhouette); © Qing Ding/ Shutterstock, **6**; © Andrea Leone/Shutterstock, **13**; © Brent Reeves/Shutterstock, **3**, **19**; © Viki & Maki/Shutterstock, **8** (seal silhouette); Tim Stenton, **11**; Taronga Zoo/Rick Stevens, **28**, **29**; Welsh Mountain Zoo, **14**, **16**, **17**, **20**; Zoo Vienna, **15**.

Many zoos helped in the creation of this book. The authors would especially like to thank ZooParc de Beauval, France, Borås Djurpark Zoo, Sweden, Welsh Mountain Zoo, Wales, Zoo Vienna, Austria, and Taronga Zoo, Australia.

While every care has been taken to trace and acknowledge copyright, the publisher tenders their apologies for any accidental infringement where copyright has proved untraceable. Where the attempt has been unsuccessful, the publisher welcomes information that would redress the situation.

Contents

When a word is printed in **bold**, you can look up its meaning in the Glossary on page 31.

Zoos

Zoos are places where people can see a lot of different animals. The animals in a zoo come from all around the world.

People can visit zoos to see animals from other parts of the world.

Zoos have special **enclosures** for each different type of animal. Some enclosures are like the animals' homes in the **wild**. They have trees for climbing and water for swimming.

Animals that swim, such as otters, need water in their enclosures.

Seals and Sea Lions

Seals are **mammals** with flippers and **streamlined** bodies. They live in and near water. Sea lions are a type of eared seal. Eared seals have ears you can see.

ear

short fur

streamlined body

large front flipper

back flippers used for walking

Eared seals use their four flippers to walk on land.

The other main type of seal is the earless seal.
Earless seals have ears that you cannot see.

small front flipper

back flippers not used for walking

streamlined body

An earless seal shuffles along the ground like a caterpillar.

In the Wild

In the wild, most seals and sea lions live in cold areas near coastlines. Most live in small groups, called pods or herds.

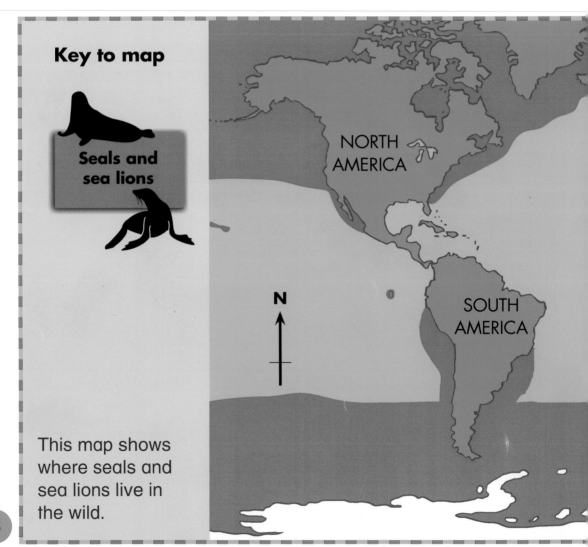

Key to map

Seals and sea lions

NORTH AMERICA

N

SOUTH AMERICA

This map shows where seals and sea lions live in the wild.

Seals and sea lions spend most of their lives in water. They eat fish, squid, and **krill**. They go to the surface of the water to breathe.

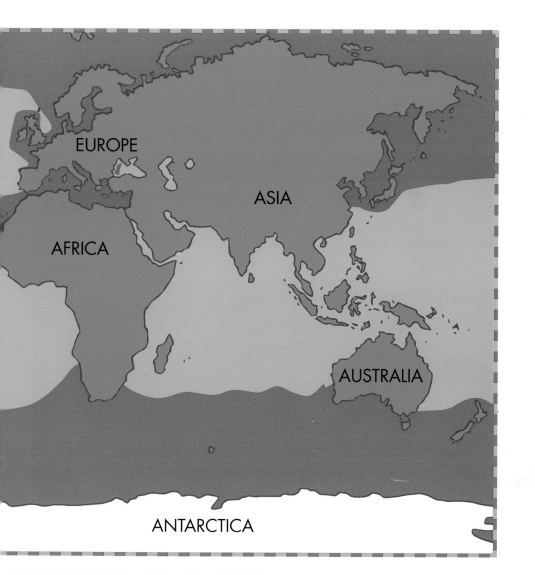

EUROPE

ASIA

AFRICA

AUSTRALIA

ANTARCTICA

Threats to Survival

The biggest threat to survival for seals and sea lions is hunting. They are hunted for their **pelts**, **blubber**, and meat.

Fewer than one thousand Hawaiian monk seals survive in the wild because of hunting.

Sometimes, seals get trapped in fishing nets and old ropes floating in the sea. Seals cannot breathe underwater, so they drown in the nets.

This seal has been tangled in a fishing net.

Zoo Homes

In zoos, seals and sea lions live in enclosures. The enclosures include deep swimming pools. The seals and sea lions like to dive down into the water.

deck for resting   deep lake for swimming

Boras Zoo, in Sweden, has a very deep natural lake for its fur seals.

The temperature of a zoo's pool needs to suit the type of seal or sea lion. Seals from cold places need pools with cold water. Some sea lions need warmer water.

This cold-water pool is for seals from cold places.

Zoo Food

In zoos, seals and sea lions are fed dead fish. Keepers add vitamins to the fish. This is to make sure the animals stay healthy.

Zoo Food for Seals and Sea Lions
fish
squid and octopus
salt
vitamins

A zookeeper cuts up fish and adds vitamins.

Feeding

Seals and sea lions are fed two or three times a day. At feeding time, keepers throw whole dead fish to each seal.

Seals leap for the food held by the zookeeper.

Zoo Health

Zookeepers look after the seals and sea lions so they stay healthy. The water in their swimming pools must be kept clean. **Veterinarians**, or vets, check each animal's health.

A zookeeper checks a sea lion's flipper for injuries.

Seals and sea lions are very intelligent. They are trained to open their mouths while vets and zookeepers check their teeth. They also shuffle onto scales to be weighed.

A sea lion opens its mouth so the zookeeper can check its teeth.

Baby Seals and Sea Lions

Seals and sea lions usually have one baby, called a pup, at a time. It takes between eight and fifteen months for a pup to grow inside its mother.

A sea lion pup is born with a thick coat of fur.

The mother gives birth to the pup on land. Some pups can swim after just a few hours. Other pups stay on land until they are strong enough to swim.

A mother harbor seal stays with her pup almost all the time.

How Zoos Are Saving Seals and Sea Lions

Zoos help save sick and injured seals. Some seal pups that have lost their parents are cared for in zoos.

A rescued seal pup is cared for by a zookeeper.

The zookeepers look after the pups until they are healthy and strong. When the pups put on weight, they may be released back into the wild.

Zookeepers return a fur seal to its home in the wild.

Zoos Working Together

Some zoos swap animals. Two male fur seals cannot live in the same enclosure because they may fight. One needs to be moved to another enclosure or zoo.

It is important not to have more than one male fur seal in an enclosure.

Some female fur seals at Boras Zoo, in Sweden, were born in other European zoos. The zoo is working with other zoos to find a male fur seal to join them.

Many of the seals at Boras Zoo come from different zoos around the world.

Meet Carlos, a Seal Keeper

Carlos is a zookeeper who works with seals.

Question	How did you become a zookeeper?
Answer	I was working with animals in movies when I was offered a job training eagles at a zoo.
Question	How long have you been a zookeeper?
Answer	I have been a zookeeper for more than twenty-two years.

Carlos feeds the sea lions in their enclosure.

Question	What animals have you worked with?
Answer	I have worked with eagles, bears, seals, and big cats.
Question	What do you like about your job?
Answer	I love being able to teach animals to understand what you want them to do.

A Day in the Life of a Zookeeper

Zookeepers have jobs to do every day. Often, a team of zookeepers work together to look after the seals and sea lions at a zoo.

9:00 a.m.
Feed the seals and then clean the feeding area.

10:30 a.m.
Check the seals to make sure they are healthy.

1:00 p.m.

Give the seals toys to play with.

3:30 p.m.

Perform in the sea lion show for visitors.

Zoos Around the World

There are zoos all around the world. Taronga Zoo, in Australia, keeps sea lions, fur seals, and leopard seals.

Taronga Zoo is home to Michi, an Australian sea lion.

Taronga Zoo's seals were injured or stranded in the wild. The zoo has created a special enclosure for them. The enclosure is like the seals' **habitat** in the wild.

The enclosure at Taronga Zoo has water and rocky areas.

The Importance of Zoos

Zoos do very important work. They:

- help people learn about animals
- save **endangered** animals and animals that are badly treated

Zookeepers feed endangered stellar sea lions.

Glossary

blubber   Layer of fat under the skin of a sea mammal, such as a seal or whale.

enclosures   The fenced-in areas where animals are kept in zoos.

endangered   At high risk of dying out and disappearing from Earth.

habitat   Area in which an animal is naturally found.

krill   Tiny, shelled animals that live in the sea.

mammals   A group of animals, such as pandas and seals, that have fur or hair, and feed their young with their own milk.

pelts   The furry skins of dead animals.

streamlined   Shaped for moving quickly through the water.

veterinarians   Animal doctors.

wild   Natural areas, such as forests, that are untouched by humans.

Index